Harry Potter™, Gryffindor™ House

Ron Weasley™, Gryffindor House

Rubeus Hagrid™

Professor Severus Snape™

Professor Albus Dumbledore™

Harry and Ron fly to Hogwarts™

Harry and Ron are about to crash

Gryffindor Vs Slytherin™

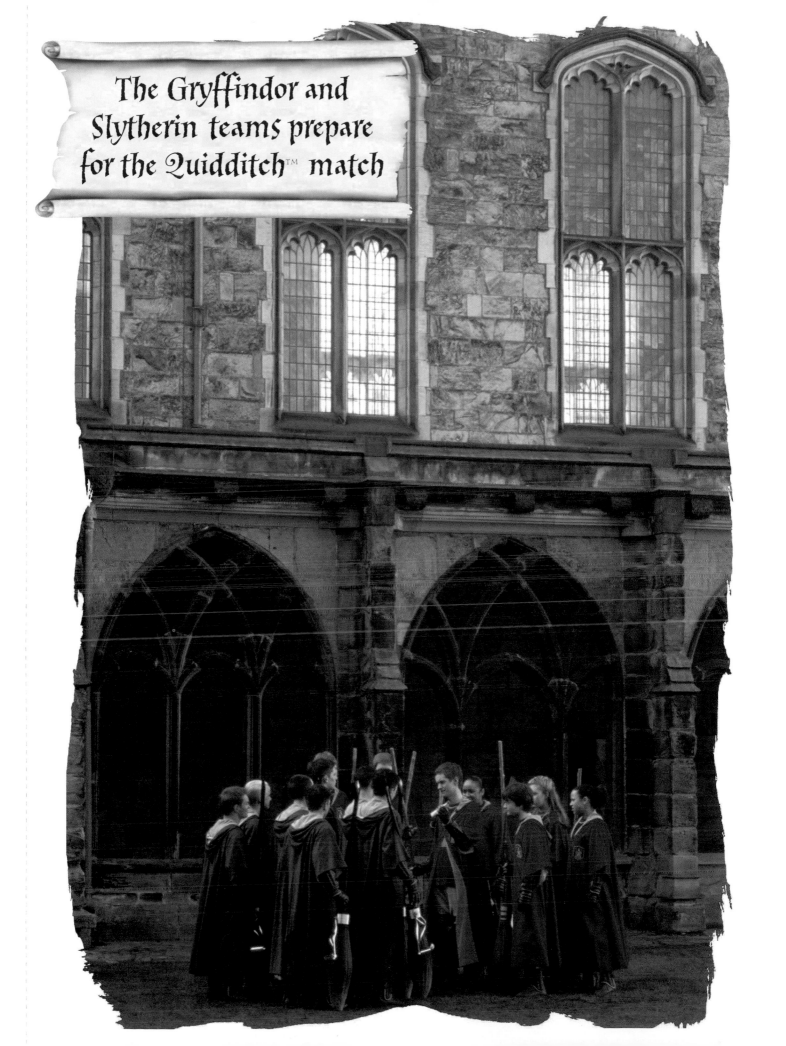

The Gryffindor and Slytherin teams prepare for the Quidditch™ match

Harry plays Quidditch for Gryffindor

Gilderoy Lockhart's™ Defence Against the Dark Arts class

Hermione asks about the legend of the Chamber of Secrets™

Filch blames Harry for the fate of Mrs Norris

Ron's broken wand

Harry overhears a group of Hufflepuffs™ talking about him

Malfoy, Crabbe and Goyle in the Slytherin Common Room

Draco Malfoy™ wonders who the Heir of Slytherin could be

Draco and Harry at the Duelling Club

Harry uses his magical powers

Harry speaks Parseltongue to stop the snake

Harry, Hermione and Ron in Moaning Myrtle's™ bathroom

Harry, Ron and Fang in the Forbidden Forest

Christmas at Hogwarts™

Harry, Ron and
Hermione and the
Polyjuice Potion™

Harry and Ron visit Hermione in the hospital wing

Harry with Tom Riddle's™ diary

Harry reads Tom Riddle's diary